Forew...	VII
This is ...	1
How H... ...ed Wonders	5
Levitation	8
Practical Levitation	11
Herrmann's Secret	19
No Support At All	27
Levitation: Yet Another Method	32
Cross-legged Levitation	34
Illusions Using Mirrors	37
Sawing A Lady Into Two	42
The Disappearing Lady	45
Jack of Hearts	48
The Indian Rope Trick	53
Before We Stop	57

Other titles by Sri M

- Shunya - A Novel
- On Meditation
- The Home Coming & Other Stories
- Yoga also for the Godless
- Apprenticed to a Himalayan Master A Yogi's Autobiography
- The Little Guide to Greater Glory and a Happier Life
- Wisdom of the Rishis
  Ishavasya, Kena, Mandukya
- Jewel in the Lotus
  Deeper Aspects of Hinduism
- How to Levitate and other Great Secrets of Magic
  by James Talbot (Sri M)
- The Upanishads
  Katha, Prashna, Mundaka
- The Journey Continues
  Sequel to Apprenticed to a Himalayan Master

Translations available of Sri M's autobiography:

- Hindi
- Telugu
- Bengali
- Spanish
- Marathi
- Malayalam
- Tamil
- Japanese
- Oriya
- Kannada
- Gujarati
- German
- Russian
- Italian

To buy books, DVD's and Digital downloads online visit www.magentapress.in

How to Levitate
and Other Great Secrets of Magic

HOW TO LEVITATE
and Other Great Secrets of Magic

By
Sri M

Magenta Press

©The author, 2013.
Sri M

First Published - 2013
Second Reprint - 2022

All rights reserved.
No part of this publication may be reproduced, stored in
re- trivial system or transmitted by any means, electronic,
photocopying, recording, or otherwise, without the prior
written permission of the copyright holders.

ISBN : 978-93-82585-02-2

Book design: J. Menon. www.grantha.com

Price: Rs.149.00.

Published by:
Magenta Press and Publication Pvt.Ltd.
No.9 | 1st Floor | Webster's Road | Cox Town
Bengaluru - 560005
info@magentapress.in | www.magentapublication.com
Ph: +91 6363083590 | 9343071537

Foreword

The starlit sky is magical; the silvery moon gliding out of the clouds is magical; the great trees, the beautiful birds, the rain, the earth painted green with lush vegetation, the moving sand dunes in the vast desert, a little child's smile — in short, all things in this world conjured up by the invisible hand of the master conjurer are magical.

To conjure up something from nothing and make something disappear into thin air is the great art of the magician. Having studied magic under various magicians and researched deep into the subject, I lay bare the secrets of magic for the reader to enjoy.

The young and the old love magic and would be delighted to figure out how these mysterious feats are performed on stage.

Last but not the least, it would help to steer clear of pretenders who expertly perform magic tricks and *claiming that they are miracles, hoodwink the public. The false has to be eliminated before the true is revealed.*

So read on and mystify your friends by levitating or producing rabbits out of a hat.

— Sri M

This is Real Magic

Hundreds of books have been written on magic and thousands of readers have eagerly gone through them in the hope of finding the secrets of great magical feats like levitation (floating in the air), sawing a lady into two pieces and restoring her again and so on. All they generally learn, is either how to make handkerchiefs disappear, find a selected card from a pack of cards and such other sleight of hand tricks; or a lot of stuff about ceremonial magic, black magic, psychic powers and so on which rarely, if ever, can be demonstrated practically. The result is that these great illusions remain closely guarded secrets known only to professional magicians.

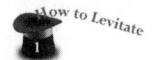

The attempt, here, is to explain these great magic tricks clearly, giving step-by-step instructions on how to perform them as effectively as professionals do. It is not the intention of the author either to prove or disprove the existence of psychic powers. This is a practical book on real magic and not one dealing with the obscure and uncertain world of occult phenomena. However, once the secret of the magical feats which are generally given supernatural explanations are discovered, readers who wish to investigate supernatural phenomenon would be better equipped to judge whether a given phenomenon of magical happening, needs any occult agency at all.

Certainly, an expert magician needs to know a great deal of human psychology and may have to depend upon the hypnotic effects of special music, exotic stage settings, personal magnetism etc., however well-equipped, he is with excellent gadgets. He should also be a glib talker and know how to handle the audience.

This does not mean that a stage magician needs to know the art of actually hypnotising a subject. In none of the great illusions, including levitation, is hypnosis made use of. When the audience sees the magician, making passes over his assistant, he is merely pretending to hypnotise. Unless of course, the fascination experienced by a large chunk of the spectators is put down to a mild form of hypnosis.

The methods described here are taken from various sources. The aspiring magician need not confine himself to the very same techniques. Once acquainted with the basics, it would be possible for him to innovate or even invent entirely new techniques for a given effect, or even build up his own original illusions which he may keep a closely guarded secret until someone else discovers it.

The reader who does not want to practise magic but who merely wishes to satisfy his curiosity, would find that, far from losing interest in a magic performance, he would enjoy it much more than when he was ignorant of the secrets. He would learn to appreciate how, although using the simplest of means, the adroit conjurer manages to spin a web of such mystery and magic that he himself, even after knowing the explanation, begins to wonder, if the secret was really so simple.

Before we go to the next chapter, it must be said that the reader who wishes to learn coin tricks, handkerchief tricks, card tricks and such ordinary sleight of hand effects will not find much here. For such readers, there are scores of books in the market.

This book goes directly to the greater illusions. It is however suggested, especially for the benefit of those who wish to be practising magicians, that they acquaint themselves with the elementary books on magic, learn as many small tricks as possible, practise them to perfection, try them out and when they are sure of themselves, add the great illusions which are dealt with here, to their repertoire.

Every magic show consists of a number of smaller tricks which in themselves are quite fascinating and entertaining and some even as baffling as the great illusions. A few great illusions usually come at the end. Therefore, readers who wish to perform on stage would do well to learn the smaller tricks from other sources. This would also in general, make them familiar with the art of spectator-handling, an art which is of utmost importance when performing the big time tricks.

Many modern day magical gadgets are pretty expensive, but inexpensive ones can often be used. There are also great effects, which can be brought about, using nothing more than two broom sticks and a sheet. One such levitation (floating in the air trick), which even a school boy can learn to perform in less than ten minutes, is also included in this book.

Sharpen your brains now. We enter the world of illusions.

How Houdini Worked Wonders

Harry Houdini was perhaps the most famous magician in history. Apart from great illusions like making an elephant appear suddenly on stage and disappear just as quickly, Houdini specialised in escapology. He could escape from the most securely locked trunks, even if they were underwater. Opening handcuffs was to him child's play. This remarkable ability to pick the most complicated locks is attributed to him having apprenticed with a locksmith during his teens, but Houdini had that peculiar quality so essential to a magician — showmanship, without which he would have died an unknown locksmith.

We will discuss one of Houdini's famous escapes now, as it will benefit the reader immensely to see how subtly he worked. First, the effect:

In 1898, whilst touring Chicago with the Welsh Brother's Circus, Houdini volunteered to escape from a police prison cell into which he was to be put after being handcuffed, with regulation police handcuffs. The local police agreed, but to make sure that there were no duplicate keys smuggled into the cell, they had Houdini stripped of all his clothes before entering the cell.

A few minutes after everybody left him securely locked up, Houdini did the impossible. He escaped and joined the police for a cup of coffee in the adjoining room. The police were amazed and the newspapers provided a lot of publicity, a commodity much desired by magicians.

Granted, that he had a skeleton key or a master key, with which he could, expert locksmith that he was, pick any lock, however there still remained the question of where he had hidden it, considering that he was naked. Two explanations have been offered. One is that the skeleton key was passed into his mouth from his wife's mouth when she gave him a parting, good luck kiss. The other is that Houdini had the skeleton key stuck with surgical tape under his foot, a place no one normally checks, especially when a person stands bare-foot.

There is no reason why both methods could not have worked, if properly stage managed. A duplicate key can easily be made by surreptitiously getting an impression of the original key, some time before the date of the performance, on a piece of beeswax, held hidden in the magician's palm, while he pretends to examine the keys which are used to lock him up. What is required, are nimble fingers and convincing conversation. For an expert locksmith like Houdini, it would have been a simple matter to make a duplicate key from a wax impression.

One more method could have been used - bribing the police, but we will not dwell on that possibility for even a second as it would be tantamount to throwing suspicion on that honest body of law and order keepers, the Chicago police.

Feats, like the one described above, are the stuff legends are made of. No wonder, Houdini became a legend. In fact, such a legend, that Sir Arthur Conan Doyle, the creator of Sherlock Holmes, who unlike his logical and rational creation, was a firm believer in the supernatural, insisted that there must be an occult explanation to many of Houdini's illusions, despite Houdini's assurance that they were all clever tricks, which required substantial physical effort.

Having come this far we will now take up levitation – the professed ability of a magician to float or cause his assistant to float in the air, apparently defying gravity.

Levitation
(Remaining suspended in the air)

The supposed ability to defy gravity and remain suspended in the air, either with the support of merely a slender rod or with no support at all, has fascinated mankind for centuries. Many accounts of levitation performed by great magicians in India, Tibet, China, Egypt and other places have been brought to the West by travellers. Some saints have also been reported to have levitated when in a deep ecstatic trance. We have no way of confirming these purported levitations. For all one knows, they may have been fantasies or exaggerations built around deftly demonstrated acrobatics.

Herrmann's Feat

However, one of the first persons to demonstrate levitation on the stage in front of hundreds of spectators was the great magician, Herrmann. Herrmann's feat was described by witnesses as follows:

A lady assistant was put into a trance-like state by Herrmann, using what he called 'ether'. Then she wa

Fig. 1

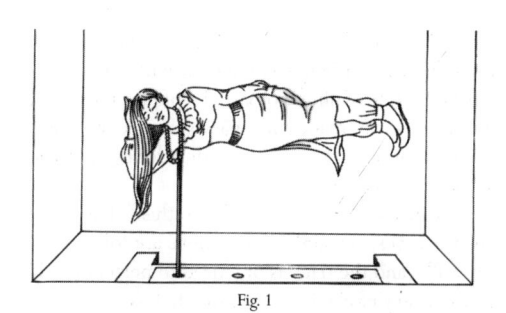

lifted up and her right armpit was made to rest on the tip of a slender, white coloured rod, which was planted on the stage. With the orchestra playing sad, weird music, Herrmann clad in impeccable evening dress, made a few passes with his hands and moved away slowly, leaving the lovely lady floating horizontally in the air with only the thin rod supporting her armpit (figure 1).

The spectators watched in silent fascination, but what made them gasp was the second part of the same illusion. Suddenly, the lights were dimmed. The orchestra stopped playing. In the dim light, the spectators could clearly see the white-clad lady suspended on the thin rod. Quietly, Herrmann walked up to her and removed the meagre support – the rod, and there she was, suspended in mid-air with no support whatsoever. In a minute or two, he put back the rod, lifted her down, made a few passes to wake her up, and both of them, bowed to the thundering applause as the curtains slowly fell.

If you ask, "Will I be able to do this?" The answer is yes, certainly, if directions are followed carefully, and the trick is practised to perfection. It is not a very easy trick, but nevertheless, you can do it. However, before you attempt a feat which Herrmann himself took years to perfect, try another method which is so simple that you'll marvel at the ease with which an audience can be fooled.

Now, mark you, when I said simple I only meant that the technique was simple. How you present it is a different matter altogether and everything depends on that. First, the effect as it appears to the spectators.

Practical Levitation

The magician puts his assistant into a deep trance and lays him on a wooden bench. Then he covers him with a large sheet up to his neck, leaving only his face uncovered. The lights are dimmed slightly, and to the accompaniment of slow, soft music, the assistant rises horizontally at a command from the magician and appears to be on the verge of floating away. He rises to about three and half to four feet in the air, above the bench and remains suspended there for a minute or two (figure 6). Then, as the magician beckons, the body descends again and goes back into the original position. The magician then wakes him up. The assistant gets up, smiles, bows and withdraws.

The Secret

All the props you need for this trick are two slender poles, like the ones used for broom sticks, which should be long enough to reach from the shoulders to the feet of the assistant who is to levitate, two small pieces of plywood (figure 2), a large thick sheet (not the thin, transparent variety) and a narrow bench for the assistant to lie on.

Cut the plywood pieces into the shapes of a shoe sole, taking care that their size is about the same as that of your assistant's feet. Then, fix them strongly using nails and glue to one end of each stick. The assistant is, of course, your confederate and not just any body called from the audience. If you and your assistant are good actors, you can make it appear as if you called in a stranger to assist you. This technique of using your own assistant, and at the same time allowing the spectators to believe that you have called in one of them, has been used by magicians for many a trick (figures 3 & 4).

The general procedure for this is as follows, but you can invent your own method to suit the trick.

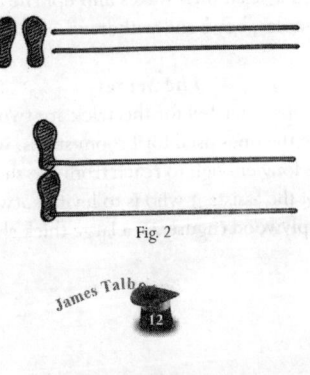

Fig. 2

The magician walks to the front of the stage and says, "Ladies and gentlemen, the next item I am going to perform is rather difficult. I need your help and co-operation."

"Can one of you volunteer to be mesmerised? I would prefer a young boy to volunteer, please."

If his assistant is a young girl, already sitting amongst the audience, he would say, "Can a young girl, please volunteer?" He continues, "mesmerism is a trifle dangerous, but I assure you that I'll try and not mesmerise you deeply."

Normally, few people volunteer. The magician's assistant, also waits to be persuaded. He may stand up or take a few steps, stop and then walk back to his seat. Then, the magician pretends to persuade him, "Sir, come on. Don't be afraid. Yes, come, come. You'll be alright." He then walks down and leads him by the hand to the stage. The assistant keeps looking back, as if he is reluctant to go. At this point, if others volunteer, the magician just ignores them. If one or two insist on coming on stage, he eliminates all of them by what he claims are tests designed to see how well they can be mesmerised. Actually, he merely asks them to close their eyes or some such thing, touches them on some part of their head or chest and says,

Fig. 3

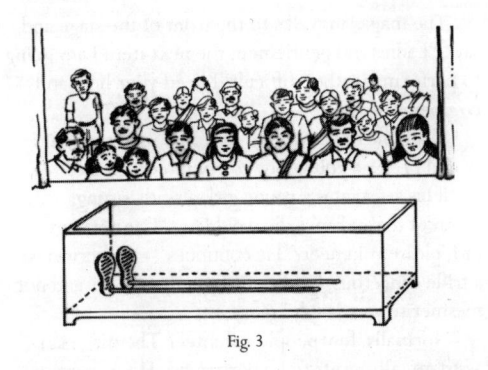

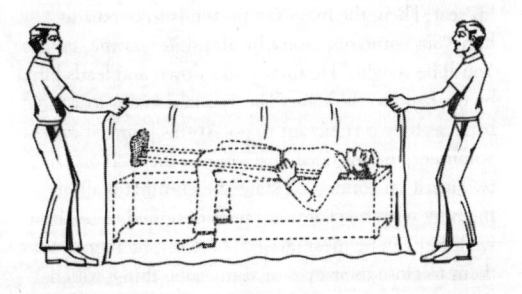

Fig. 4

James Talbot
14

"I am afraid you have bad reactions," and sends them back.

Once his assistant is on stage, both he and the magician act as if they are total strangers. The magician asks him his name and other particulars, before asking him to lie down on the bench. The bench is already in the middle of the stage, draped in a sheet that covers it completely. The other alternative is a bench made like a box, with only the side which is away from the audience being left open.

The assistant first sits on the bench and then stretches himself on it. Two other assistants appear with a large sheet. For a minute or two, they hold the sheet like a curtain in front of the bench on which the subject is lying, and pretend to adjust it properly. It is in this short interval of time, that the subject, now totally hidden from the spectators, picks up the sticks and lies down again with his legs folded at the knees and feet firmly planted on the floor, on either side of the bench, holding the sticks in such a way, that the plywood cut outs are where his feet should have been. He holds the sticks firmly with his hands (figure 4).

As soon as he is ready, which with sufficient practice, takes half a minute or less, the assistants cover

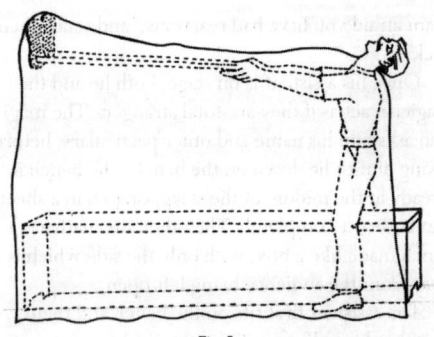

Fig. 5

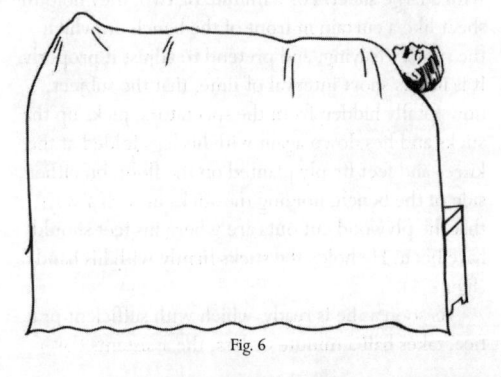

Fig. 6

James Talbot

him with the sheet, leaving only his face and head uncovered. Now, with the lights dimmed, for effect and to the accompaniment of soft music, he has only to keep his head horizontal to the floor and carefully stand up in slow motion, making sure that the sticks are also held parallel to the floor. This requires a little practice. The sheet should also be properly adjusted so that it does not slip off. The result, if properly performed, is astounding. The spectators see the person levitating and it appears as if he would float away from the stage (figure 5).

A warning: Do not overdo it. In a minute or two, give the command to descend. When the sheet is pulled up from one side by the assistants, the levitator, once more, under the cover for a few seconds, puts back the sticks and resumes his supine position with his legs stretched on the bench. The magician pretends to wake him up from his trance. He gets up and totters away, giving the appearance of being only half awake. The magician thanks him profusely.

A word of caution – ensure that the sheet is long and broad enough to cover the feet even when the assistant stands up to his full height. The bench should be as narrow as possible to enable the assistant to place his feet on either side without discomfort. This trick can also be performed with the feet resting on the bench, instead of the floor, but this would mean that the assistant would appear to levitate at a lower height, which is the maximum elevation possible when he sits up.

Herrmann's Secret

The following is the secret of Herrmann's feat described at the start of this chapter. The rod in figure 7, should be sturdy enough to support the weight of a not too heavy human body. It is made from iron or steel and is fixed to a heavy wooden stand as shown in figure 7. To avoid letting the audience know that the stand is heavy, it is brought before hand and placed behind a small curtain, at centre stage. When the magician begins his act, the curtain is pulled aside.

Some magicians make use of mechanical devices to hold the rod in place steadily, instead of using the kind of permanently fixed rod and stand unit, so

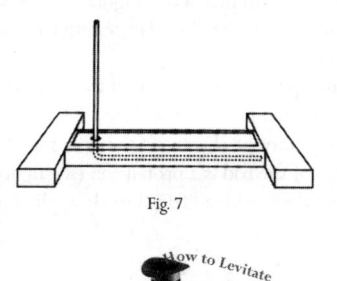

Fig. 7

that the rod can be brought in and fixed to the stand anytime. The kind of unit described in figure 7 is preferable as it is fool proof.

Invariably, for this illusion, the magician uses his own assistant, usually, a beautiful girl, well-made up and wearing oriental robes. She certainly cannot wear a tight dress, as the secret of levitation, lies in the folds of her costume. There are many complicated gadgets for levitation, involving a system of gears but the simple one, which is described below, is as good as any other. Once the secret is revealed, it is hoped that mechanical minded readers, invent their own versions.

Inside her robes, the lady assistant straps on the device shown in figure 9. It consists of a not too heavy metal shell, shaped to accommodate the contours of lady assistant's body and covers half her body on both sides (see figures 8 and 8A). On the back portion, on level with the arm pits, a rectangular sheath is welded on (see figure 8A, detail 1). The sheath has a small slit near its closed end.

A small part of the top end of the rod, which is fixed to the stand, is also flattened so that it can slide effortlessly into the sheath. At the very top of the flattened end of the rod is a protrusion (see figure 8A, detail 2), which with a little cleverly applied pressure

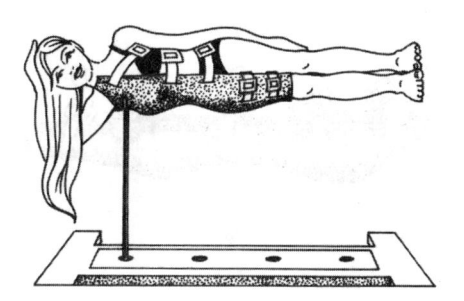

Fig. 8

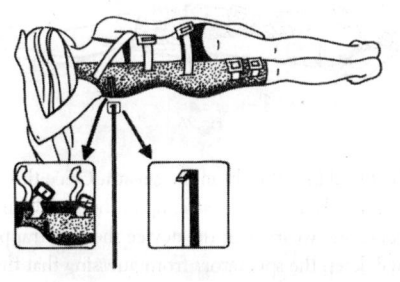

Fig. 8A

How to Levitate

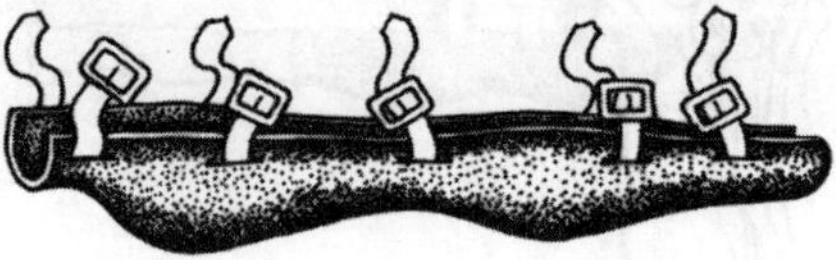

Fig. 9

Fig. 9A

can be fitted into the slit in the sheath. Once this is done, the lady assistant is safe, up in the air. The flowing robes she wears over the device she has strapped on, will keep the spectators from guessing that the rod is not actually supporting her armpit.

Another Method

Another method is to have a hollow pipe instead of a rod, as in figure 7 and instead of a protruding sheath as in figure 8A, detail 1, have a rod of about two or three inches in length, welded on to the shell. The rod should be slipped into the pipe to support the shell and the person who wears it. To prevent the rod from revolving inside the pipe or slipping out of it, a tiny bolt is slipped in through holes a, b, c, d, drilled in a straight line and passing through the centre of the pipe as well as the rod (figure 10, detail). The bolt is shot by the magician after his assistants have lifted the lady to the correct position, so that the holes are all aligned properly. The author has tried this method and found it quite successful.

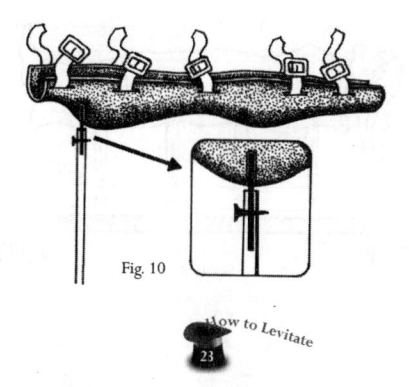

Fig. 10

Three Sword Levitation

The same method is adopted but with a little difference. The assistant lies flat on the points of three swords as shown in figure 10 A. Swords two and three are removed and the assistant levitates seemingly on the point of one sword - sword number 1.

The difference is that the shell is made to accommodate the back portion of the assistant's body and a metal sheath is welded to it. The pointed end of sword number 1 enters the sheath to a length of three inches, which is sufficient to hold the weight of the assistant. The costume as in the previous tricks covers up the protruding sheath. Needless to mention, sword number one is either permanently fixed to the stand, like the rod in the other levitation trick

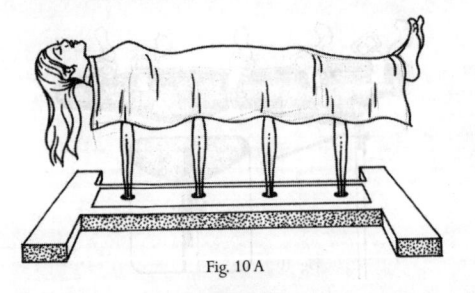

Fig. 10 A

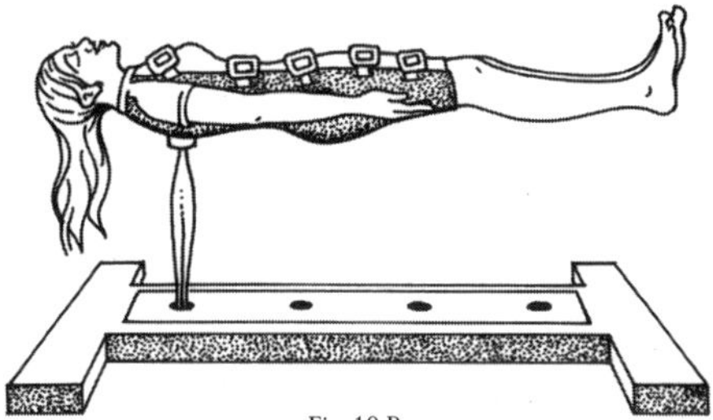

Fig. 10 B

or some arrangement is made, so that it does not fall whilst bearing the weight of the body (figure 10 B).

Pulling Out the Support

One question remains unanswered. How did the great Herrmann pull out even the single rod which supported the lady and leave her suspended in mid-air?

He was only making use of the fact known to most magicians, that when the lights are not so bright, black objects placed in front of a black screen are not visible to the human eye from a certain distance. The black screen, as well as the objects should not be polished or shiny, so that the possibility of the light being reflected is eliminated. So silk, plastic and other glistening materials are ruled out. Black velvet screens are however quite good for the purpose. The objects should also be painted with black paint, with a dull finish or covered with the same kind of black cloth used for the background.

When Herrmann pulled out the rod, he was only pulling out a white plastic shell, which covered the actual supporting rod. The supporting rod was painted black and hence was not visible when in front of the black curtains. The spectators were under the impression that the supporting rod was white and that, Herrmann had pulled it out at the last minute. The dim lights contributed to the success of this illusion.

The modern day magician, instead of dim lights, uses ultra-violet lamps for such illusions. All the objects, which are to remain invisible to the spectators, are painted black. The back and side curtains are also black. The objects, which are to be clearly visible to the spectators are treated with fluorescent paint. The make-up, which the magician and his assistants wear, and all their costumes are treated with fluorescent paint, which makes them appear clear and bright against a black background when ordinary lights are turned off.

No Support At All

One of the illusions in which modern magicians make use of ultraviolet lights and fluorescent paint is the levitation trick described below.

The magician hypnotizes the lady assistant and carries her in his arms. A curtain in the middle of the stage is then drawn open, and reveals two assistants, holding a white tray as shown in figure 11. The background is black, of course. The magician walks up to the tray and lays down the lady on it. The normal lights are switched off and the ultraviolet lights turned on. At a signal from the magician, his assistants remove the tray and take is away. The lady remains suspended in mid-air (figure 12).

Holding a ring, the magician takes it all the way from the head of the suspended lady, to her legs and back again, a couple of times, to prove that there are no hidden supports of any kind. In a minute or two, the assistants, come back with the tray and place it under the lady's body. The magician awakens the assistant from her trance, she waves and walks away.

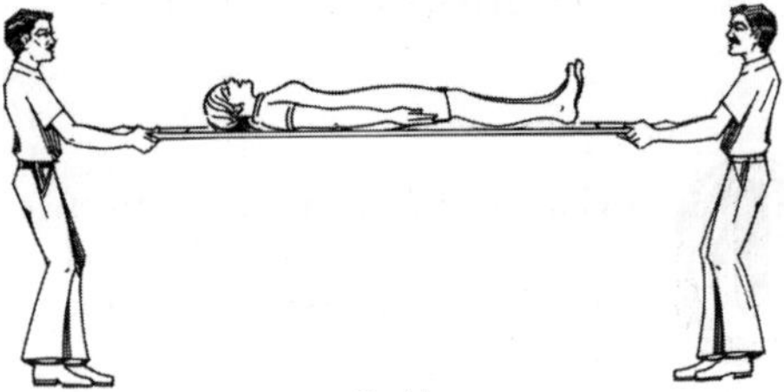

Fig. 11

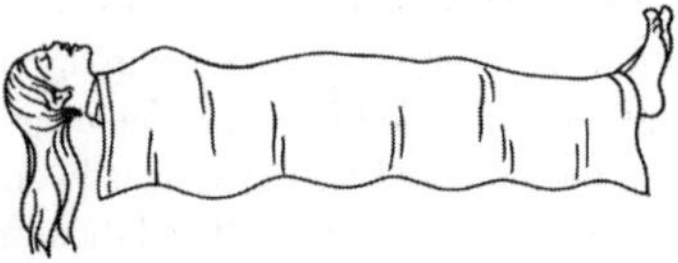

Fig. 12

The Secret

The lady assistant wears a shell of the type worn in the Three Sword Levitation. However, there is a difference. The sheath is of a different kind (figure 13) and is located at a different point, so that the body is properly balanced. From a hole in the black curtain comes a rod, which is painted black and flattened at the end, so that it can enter the sheath smoothly. This rod is fixed securely to a heavy stand placed behind the curtain and so constructed that it can bear the weight of the floating lady (figure 14).

The assistants, holding the white tray are there, only to hide the support. The tray in figure 15 has only one side-wall, on the side, facing the spectators. As soon as the support has been slid into the sheath, the tray is removed, the normal lights turned off and the ultraviolet lights are switched on. Again, flowing

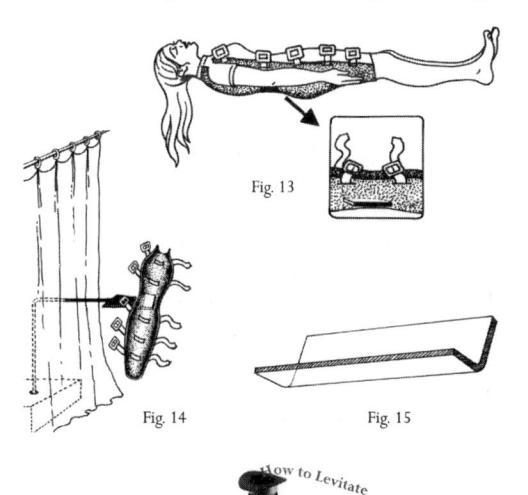

Fig. 13

Fig. 14

Fig. 15

Fig. 16

robes conceal the shell that the lady wears. The costumes of the magician and his assistants and the tray are all treated with fluorescent paint, which glows when exposed to the special ultraviolet light.

Now, only one feature remains unexplained. How can a ring be passed, from head to foot of the assistant if there is a support in the centre which will obstruct the ring. The explanation (figure 16) is that, the ring is so constructed that a gap is created when necessary, by pulling gently on either side. Of course, care should be taken to see that it is not visible to the spectators.

The tray hides the supporting rod in the beginning and later, the lady's body obscures it effectively. The black against black effect, ensures that it remains invisible to the audience, whichever angle they look at it from.

Levitation: Yet Another Method

The magician lifts up a small boy or girl in his arms and holds the child horizontally in front of him. Chanting mysterious incantations for some time, he suddenly takes his arms away from the child's body. The child levitates, as if supported by a mysterious magnetic force that seems to exude from the fingers of the magician's outstretched arms held over the child (figure 17).

Fig. 17

The Secret

If you notice, the magician does not move, but remains in the same position, whilst the child is levitating, you will probably, guess where the support comes from. If he moved, the child would also move, as the support comes from the magician's own body. Different kinds of support, may be used, but all of them are basically built like the one shown in figure 18.

The frame is made of strong, flat metal strips, bent at C to hang over the magician's shoulders. The belt B goes around his waist and holds it in place. The supporting rod is folded and hidden in the folds of the robe or under the tie or even painted to look like a tie and kept folded under the original tie. The prop is worn either inside the clothes or over a shirt and then a coat worn over it.

Fig. 18

The child wears a sheathed shell under the flowing costume. It is assumed that the reader has now become expert enough to work out the details of the actual presentation.

Stimulate the brain – it can work wonders.

Cross-legged Levitation

This has nothing to do with the so called Siddhi Levitation of the TM Group, which requires the aspirant to pay quite a substantial fee, to learn the technique. Disillusioned practitioners reveal that it is only a form of hopping about in a cross-legged posture, which has given many of them a painful bottom!

The writer would like to add that any good photographer would be able to take 'what looks like a perfect photograph of levitation, using a high shutter speed, so that the hopping acolyte's picture is captured before he touches the ground. Any photographer will also tell you that it is not difficult to make a person sitting, standing or reclining in any posture, anywhere, to appear to be levitating in a photograph. Many such fake photographs have been used by mediums in the past.

What is described below is merely an illusion, a trick. No siddhi, no faked photographs.

A holy man wearing flowing robes sits on the bare floor. The disciples bring a long pole and a large blanket. A hole is dug and the pole is fixed firmly on the ground, so that about five feet of the pole is visible above the ground. The disciples, then, cover the body of the holy man with the blanket and lift him up, so that, in the same cross-legged position he is able to touch the top of the pole with his out-stretched right hand. After a few minutes, the blanket is removed and the spectators gasp, to see that the holy man is suspended in mid-air, still cross-legged, supporting himself only by touching the top of the pole, with the palm of his right hand (figure 19).

Fig. 19

The Secret
Simple enough, inside his robes is a shell, shaped like a chair, which can be attached to the strong metal tube which is hidden inside the pole (figure 20). There are many other techniques which can be used

Fig. 20

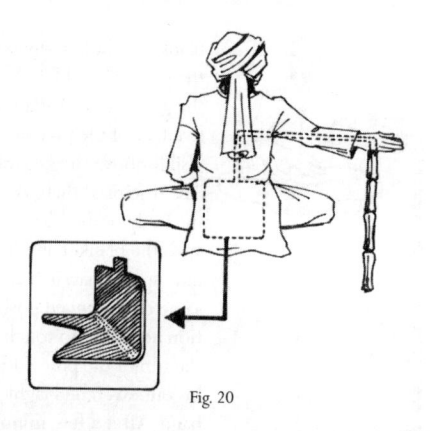

for levitation, but they are usually variations and adaptations of the technique described above. Creative magicians can invent their own techniques. Perhaps, a new method can be invented, which can use the laws of magnetic attraction and repulsion. Many a trick has been performed using magnets.

Illusions Using Mirrors

Mirrors are an integral part of a modern magician's props. In many of the big illusions, mirrors are made use of. After the reader has studied the two illusions described below, he will be in a position to invent some more. The main point to note is the proper angle at which the mirrors are to be placed.

The Talking Head

The magician walks in holding an ornamental box which he carefully places on a plain, thin topped, three legged table, in the centre of the stage.

"Ladies and gentlemen, this is a trophy I won in the mountains of Tibet. There was a Tibetan magician who challenged me to a magical duel. If I won, I could take his head away as a trophy, as if he won … well, you know what would have happened. Jokes aside, I must show you what is in the box."

He opens the front position of the box and audience gasps in horror (figure 21). There really is a human inside with closed eyes, placed on what seems

Fig. 21

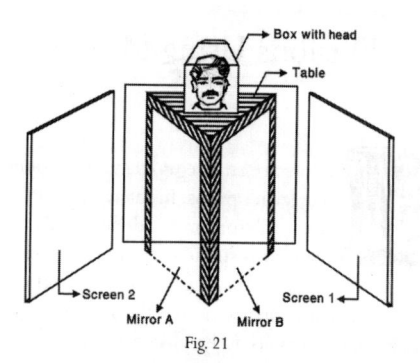

to be hay. Soon the audience wonders if it is a rubber replica of a human head. The magician quitely opens its mouth, so that the audience can see the tongue and teeth. Then he opens the eye lids, so that they can see the eyes. To top it all, he asks the head: "Whose head, may I please ask, did you belong to, before I brought you here?"

Pat comes the reply.

"The head of Mingyar Dondup, the magician, high up in Shigatze."

The magician then invites a few of the spectators to ask questions, which are answered satisfactorily. He then closes the box and takes it away.

The Secret

Under the table sits an assistant who, through a trap door in the table top, pushes his head into the box. The box also has a door at the bottom which can be pushed aside. He is not visible to the audience because between the front leg and the two rear legs of the triangular table, are fixed two mirrors A and B, which touch the floor at the bottom, and at the top, touch the underside of the table top.

These mirrors which are fitted at an angle of 90 degrees (figure 22) reflect the side screens 1 & 2. Screens 1 & 2 are decorated outside but are black on the inside and therefore it appears as if screen 3, which is at the back, is visible, though what is really

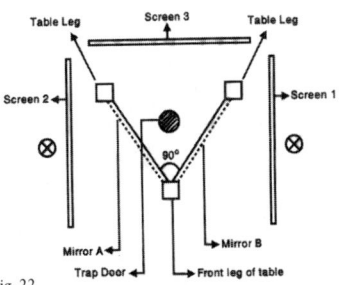

Fig. 22

visible is a reflection of 1 & 2. The spectators cannot see the assistant sitting behind the mirrors.

One precaution the magician has to take is to ensure that under no circumstances, should he come between the mirrors and the screens, because the spectators will see his legs reflected in the mirrors.

Figure 23, shows a variation of the same illusion. The head appears to be inside the box, placed on top of a broad-blade sword, laid across the arms of an upholstered armchair. A mirror is fixed at points A1 and A2 at an angle of 45 degrees from the seat. It reflects the seat of the chair C, to look like the back. The as-

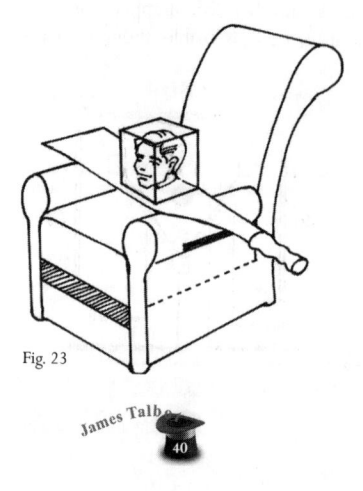

Fig. 23

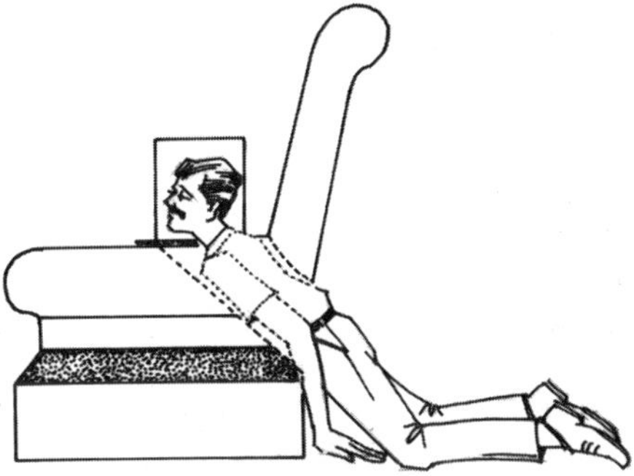

Fig. 24

sistant sits behind the chair and through, an opening in the back, pushes his head and body forward, so that he can conveniently put his head into the box (figure 24).

Now, the reader can invent his own spectacular illusions using mirrors. Assistants can be made to appear and disappear instantly and so can animals. The great Houdini used to make a live elephant disappear on stage with the help of a gigantic mirror. If you don't find elephants, you could try the same illusion with a car or motorcycle.

Sawing A Lady Into Two

A coffin with openings, at the head and foot, is laid on the table. The lid is taken off and a lady assistant climbs into it, puts her head out through one opening and her feet through the other. The lid is secured. The magician and his assistant proceed to saw the coffin through its middle with a large saw. When they have sawed it through completely, the two pieces are pulled apart, along with their severed human contents. The lady assistant's feet move, when the magician commands and so does her head (figure 25).

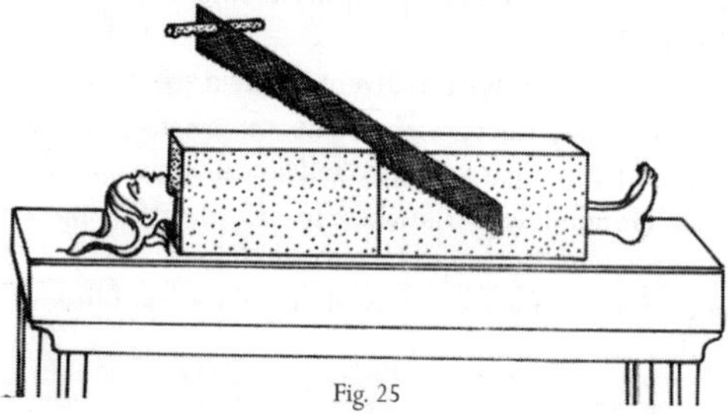

Fig. 25

The two pieces are brought back to the original position, and in minutes, when the lid of the coffin is opened, the lady steps out smiling, still in one piece.

The Secret

For the secret, look carefully, at figure 26. The table seems to have a narrow top, but that again is an illusion, created by the thin line, painted around it, in a bright colour. Since, the attention of the spectators, is fixed on the bright line, they fail to notice the thickness of the rest of the table. In the table is hidden, another lady assistant, wearing the same stockings and footwear, as the one who entered the coffin. The lady who entered, merely folds herself up, as shown

Fig. 26

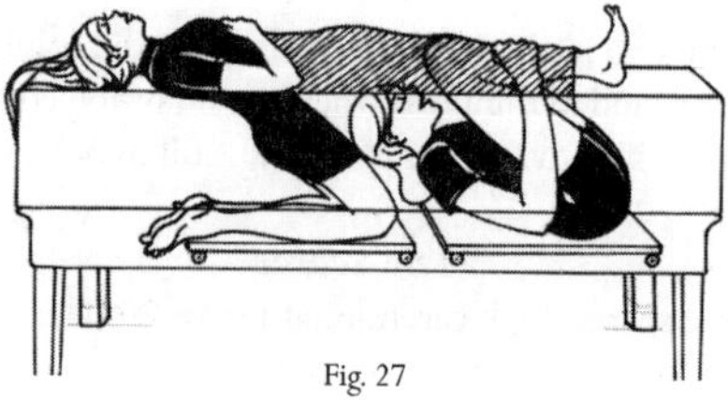

Fig. 27

in the figure, and the one inside in the table, puts her feet out through a panel in the table, and another panel at the bottom of the coffin, so that they stick out through the opening at the end of the coffin.

When the pieces of the box are pulled apart, it is the part on the left which is moved considerably because the entire body of the lady can be moved.

Sawing without a Coffin

Some modern magicians use a plastic shell and perform the trick without a coffin. Figure 27 reveals the secret of this trick. Needless to say, the girls need to be trained in the proper posture that are to adapt and the saw has to be handled carefully and accurately to avoid any accident.

The Disappearing Lady

In the middle of the stage is spread a lovely rug on which is placed a sturdy chair. A lady assistant is made to sit on it, and the magician covers her with a black shawl. Making a few passes, he quickly pulls off the shawl. The lady disappears without a trace. The magician claps his hands, and instantaneously, she walks up from the midst of spectators.

The Secret

This is one of the tricks, which makes use of a trapdoor, in the floor of the stage. Many of the modern auditoriums have removable panels, which are used for plays. The important thing for the magician is to have a duplicate panel with a trap door made, with which he replaces the original one provided in the auditorium. On this duplicate panel is pasted a rug with lovely designs, which is cut where required so that the trap door opens and shuts freely.

The trap door opens downwards, if pressure is applied from above, and operated by springs, shuts on its own accord when released. The chair is placed in such a position, that the trapdoor is directly below it. It is a specially constructed chair, whose seat slopes downward when pressure is applied.

As soon as the magician covers her with the shawl, she presses against the seat strongly, and slips down through the trap door to land softly on cushions, placed under the platform. Immediately, she makes it to one of the entrances to the auditorium and awaits the magician's call.

A frame, made of metal wire, which normally hangs behind the chair's back, is pulled over the lady's head by the magician, while he covers her with the shawl. It is this frame, which when covered by the shawl, appears to the audience like the lady's head long after she herself has slipped away.

When the magician pulls off the shawl, he makes sure that the upward movement of the shawl, throws the frame back to its original position behind the back of the chair. The design on the rug is so done that the trapdoor, once closed, is not visible from a certain distance.

Many wonderful tricks can be performed with the help of trap doors.

With two trap doors, the illusion of making a person entering one box, appear in the other, can be easily performed. Dozens of tricks can be worked out with a little imagination. But can a person appear to materialize out of thin air, as it were, even if the stage does not have a trap door? The answer is yes. The following illusion is quite spectacular and not so difficult as it might seem at first.

Jack of Hearts

The magician's assistants carry four giant sized playing cards: the jack of spades, hearts, clubs and diamonds. They turn them around and display both sides to the spectators to prove that there is nothing hidden. Then they set up the cards to form a cubicle, with the top open (figure 28).

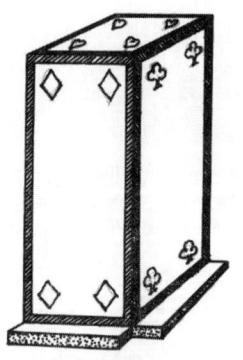

Fig. 28

The spectators are allowed to choose anyone of the jacks. In a minute, the magician pushes aside the card in front to reveal a boy dressed up as the Jack of Hearts or as the card that was chosen by the audience, just a moment ago.

The Secret

The gigantic cards are made of plywood, nailed on to a sturdy frame, with stands at the bottom to hold them up right. One of the cards which should be positioned at the rear, has a secret door with a latch and hinges cleverly concealed. It can be opened and shut both from the inside and outside.

After the cards are set up to look like a booth, another assistant walks in from behind the stage. Please note carefully, that he does not come in from the wings. He comes in from behind the curtains at the back or from the wings that are at the back. This is because he cannot afford to present his side view to the audience, since the boy who is to appear inside the booth, sits on a support that hangs from his shoulders (figure 29).

Therefore, he moves in such a way that the audience only sees his front. The assistant walks up to the magician, who stands beside the booth and hands him

Fig. 29

a black velvet bag, which is to be used for choosing the card. For a minute, he stands near the booth in the position, shown in figure 30.

It is at this moment, the boy jumps down from the support (music drowns the sound of the jump, if any), and hides behind the card at the back. Meanwhile, the magician engages the spectators in choosing the jack they want. The boy quietly opens the secret door, shuts it from inside and stands ready in the booth. He is dressed in robes which have the emblem of the card, the audience has chosen, stitched on or embroidered.

Fig. 30

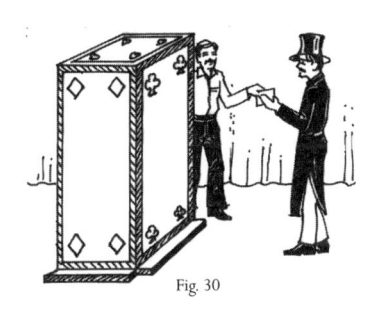

Now, the crucial question. How does the boy or the magician know which card the audience would choose? The fact is that the audience does not choose at all. Although they believe they have. The magician decides in advance which jack is to appear inside the booth, and therefore, the emblem is stitched on to the boy's costume beforehand. The magician tricks the audience into choosing the same card, he has already decided upon. This is done with a special bag, which is used in a variety of tricks by conjurors.

The bag, usually, made of black velvet and has two compartments (figure 31), made by sewing the three edges of A, B and C - three pieces of black velvet. Unknown to the spectators, one compartment contains rolled up bits of paper strips, all containing

Fig. 31

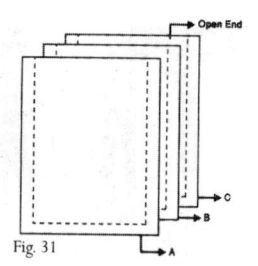

the name of the jack – for instance, the jack of hearts, which the magician, has already decided upon.

Ten spectators are each given blank strips of paper to write down their choice. These are then rolled up and put into the bag – actually, in the other compartment, which is empty. The magician then shakes the bag and opens it again, to let one spectator dip into the bag and choose one of the prepared strips from the other compartment. The magician keeps the other compartments closed with his fingers.

Naturally, whichever strip, the member of the audience picks out, contains only the name of the card, already decided upon by the magician. The rest is quite easy and needs no explanation.

The Indian Rope Trick

The great Indian rope trick is said to have been performed as follows: the magician, in his flowing robes, would throw up one end of a coil of thick rope, which has been examined by the spectators. The rope would keep ascending until only the other end touches the ground, then it would become stiff. A small, dark-skinned boy, would climb the rope, and by the time he reached the top, he would just vanish into thin air. Soon, parts of his body – arms, legs, torso and head, would fall down to the ground.

The magician, after weeping and beating his chest over the loss of the boy, would collect the parts and put them together in a basket. In a few minutes, the boy would walk out of the basket and salaam the audience. All this in the open-air, according to the accounts of ancient travellers.

Unfortunately, no modern traveller has reported this feat being performed outside, in the open-air, and the accounts of the ancient travellers tend to be exaggerated – a fault that appears in a fair number of travellers' tales — especially by westerners, who visited India or the East in general, to help add that extra touch of mystery to their oriental tales.

The rope trick can certainly be performed but not in the open. Some magicians, have performed their own versions of the rope trick on stage. The following is a version of the rope trick, which the author has himself tried with success.

The magician lets the spectators examine a thick, white cotton rope, which he coils loosely and puts in a snake-charmer's basket, which has also been examined by the audience. The lights are dimmed and as the orchestra plays the Indian snake charmer's tune, one end of the rope suddenly rises up from the basket, and climbs steadily until it disappears behind the flies.

A young boy walks in from the wings, and holds the rope as if to climb up. At the sound of a gong, he disappears right there. The rope falls down. The lights are bright again. The magician claps his hands and the boy walks in from amongst the audience.

The Secret

As the magician puts back the rope into the basket after it has been examined, he attaches an iron cap to

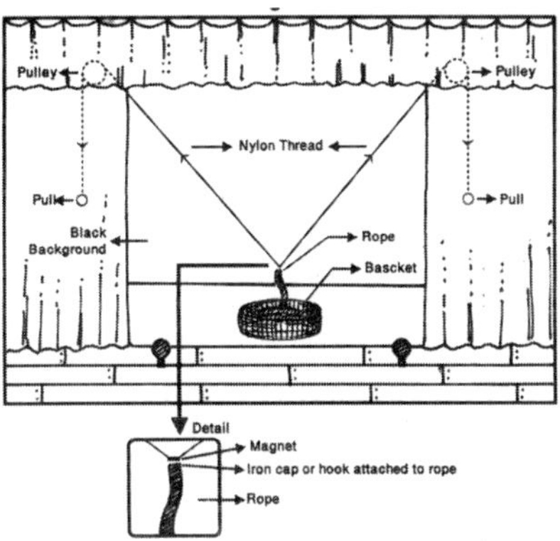

Fig. 32

one end of the rope. Off stage assistants, lower a tiny, black magnet tied to a strong nylon thread as shown in figure 32 and operated by a set of pulleys. As the magnet comes near the iron capped end of the rope, it attaches itself to it. The assistants, now pull the thread taut and the rope ascends until the top end is covered by the flies (the background is black and the lights are dim).

The boy who walks in, wears a black shield as shown in figure 33. To disappear, in dim light, in

Fig. 33

front of the black background, all he needs to do is turn around quickly, so that the audience see only the black shield (and cannot distinguish it from the black background), and walk away quickly into the wings, and from there to the auditorium, after removing the shield.

There are many other ways of performing the rope trick and the reader may invent a new technique if he or she is sufficiently serious about it.

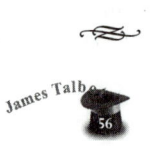

Before We Stop

Having revealed so much, the writer thinks it is time to stop. The reader who goes through this book carefully, will soon become adept at finding out the 'secret' of any illusion. When for instance, he sees a magician catch a bullet fired from a gun, he would know that the magician's assistant, must have substituted, a dummy cartridge, when loading the gun and that the used bullet, which the magician spits into the salver, was kept hidden in his mouth all the time.

So, best of luck, dear magician. Only practise your tricks to perfection before you present them, otherwise you will make a fool of yourself.

Before stopping, however, it would be worthwhile to refer briefly to another of those great tricks which magicians have tried to keep a closely guarded secret — x-ray eyes, the supposed ability to see even when blind-folded thoroughly, using dough and adhesive tape and long strips of black cloth wound around the eyes, at least a dozen times.

The writer does not want to reveal the entire secret, as he would like the reader to work it out for himself. The few hints provided below will be useful.

A well-known American magician calls it a 'peek down the nose';
The cloth used for the blindfold should definitely be black;
The more prominent your nose, the easier it is;
Dough and adhesive tape help to see better, especially if the climate is warm; and
The tighter the blind fold, the better you see.

Now, good bye and may you solve more and more mysteries and invent many more.
ABRACADABRA!!!